The Enemy

The Enemy

RAFAEL CAMPO

Duke University Press

Durham and London   2007

Printed in the United States of America on
acid-free paper ⊗

Designed by Heather Hensley

Typeset in Monotype Fournier by Tseng
Information Systems, Inc.

Library of Congress Cataloging-in-
Publication Data appear on the last printed
page of this book.

for Jorge, forever

So much of a writer's life consists of assumed suffering, rhetorical suffering, that I felt something like relief, even elation, when the doctor told me I had cancer. . . . Suddenly in the air was a rich sense of crisis — real crisis, yet one that also contained echoes of the ideas of the crisis of language, the crisis of literature, or of personality. It seemed to me that my existence, whatever I thought, felt, or did, had taken on a kind of meter, as in poetry.

ANATOLE BROYARD, *INTOXICATED BY MY ILLNESS*

The Soul unto itself
Is an imperial friend —
Or the most agonizing Spy —
An Enemy — could send —

EMILY DICKINSON

CONTENTS

IV. Dawn, New Age

ACKNOWLEDGMENTS

Grateful acknowledgment is made to the editors of the following periodicals, in which some of the poems in this book have appeared, sometimes in slightly different forms:

Bellevue Literary Review	*New Letters*
Bloom	*Nimrod*
Boston Review	*North Dakota Quarterly*
Both	*Ploughshares*
Callaloo	*Poesis*
Commonweal	*The Progressive*
Cortland Review	*River Styx*
Descant	*Seattle Review*
Euphony	*Smartish Pace*
Indiana Review	*Tiferet*
Los Angeles Review	*Virginia Quarterly Review*
Mid-American Review	*Washington Square*
The Nation	*Yale Review*

Translations from *Cien Sonetos de Amor* and *Libro de Preguntas* by Pablo Neruda first appeared in *The Poetry of Pablo Neruda*, edited by Ilan Stavans (New York: Farrar, Straus, and Giroux, 2003).

"Toward a Theory of Memory" was the 2004 Phi Beta Kappa Poem for Ohio Wesleyan University.

I. THE ENEMY

Dialogue with Sun and Poet

in memory of June Jordan

The sun is making arguments again.
Today, its dappled chattering through leaves
persuades me that the world deserves reprieve.
You're dead, and though your subjects were contained

in poetry that sometimes flustered me—
I wanted to restore some order in
your fridge, to witness Palestinian
outrage somehow more dispassionately—

I see now it was you who rewrote me.
The sun refuses any compromise,
insisting on the beauty of its rays,
like you, illuminating how we're free

yet not. Democracies of bugs and sand,
fat kingdoms of the sun, we're all
beneath what both of you, great fireballs
of life, have helped me better comprehend

as truth. It's June, too bright to be the end
of days that some foretell; the sun has more
to teach, and soldiers still have distant wars
they might imagine never starting. Instrument

of peace, I take this pen into my hand
to write, the morning almost over now.
Flood the page with light, burn the house down,
is what you say. *Arise.* I understand.

Addressed to Her (Provincetown, June 2002)

On seeing you that second time last night,
Pat Benatar a disembodied blare
amidst a night yet ravenous for dares,
I thought I'd talk to you, to ask you why

you let him grab your bangled arm that way.
Presumptuous, I thought myself, to want
to enter in your narrative of hurt.
A sparkly rhinestone necklace named you "Kaye";

your tan was richly oiled, as if burnished more
by hand than sun. A teenager flashed by,
his skateboard growling come-ons as he eyed
your heaving breasts. I wondered, too, how your

caress might feel, if not to me, then to another.
Around you glowed the plinkering arcade,
like summer carnivals where I played straight.
"Stop it—hey, you're hurting me." I smothered

her, desperate to remake myself, her body
so soft I prayed it might accept me, hold
impressions long enough to be retold
as truth. Kaye, I wanted to so badly

I made myself forget what you must know:
You turn to him, so awkwardly bent back,
too beautiful to resist, the night gone black,
and offer your unyielding, human soul

stretched taut—forgiving him, forgiving us.

"Elsa, Varadero, 1934"

Black ocean and white beach — gray sky beyond —
she clasps her wide-brimmed hat atop her head,
holding on to what she could. Even then,
invisible, such forces were at work,
roiling her dress, exerting modern will.
She turns away, but in the gusting wind
America insists on having her.
Color is not invented yet, too late
to prove to me those eyes were jungle green.
Her diamond's half-remembered glinting pink —
she isn't poor, reclining on the sand,
not yet. The photograph, despite its flat
and only half-discovered world, admits
some cause for youthful hope: gardenias dance
across her undone silken scarf, as if
they knew that someday I would notice them
and wish I'd learned her Cuban songs. That day
drops off into oblivion's dark haze,
the love of the conquered nothing if not strong.

Night Has Fallen

You would have loved the irony: The dark
persists, Reinaldo, even as
you helped to conquer it. I lost the book
of poetry, your first, found used someplace
I traveled to. (Not Cuba — maybe France,
or Spain.) That first encounter was by chance,
although I'm sure I'd seen you with the lepers —
the AIDS ward where I worked was like a shipwreck
on some lost, quarantined island. I thought
we could have been like brothers, or like lovers,
as if in poetry the world could be
made whole. By then, you were already dead
of course, but how was I to know it? Night
was falling everywhere, and everywhere
I looked I saw my own black memories;
I learned what cannot be recovered teaches.
Reinaldo, how I wish I could have called
to you before this sleeplessness set in!
I think you could have shown me love beneath
a banyan tree, then freedom stolen from
the wallet of a hypocrite, and then,
escaping fortresses' and hospitals'
white, stench-smeared walls, at last, the way back home.

Personal Mythology

That's him, the little faggot I remember,
all that hair slicked back with foamy mousse
drying hard as a helmet. There he goes,
his eyes watching his own shape in the mirror,

the outline of his half-hard dick in jeans
and the downy chest hair in the deep V
of his unbuttoned oxford places he
imagines being touched. Dumb kid, he preens

to disco music from the turntable,
some Trojans stolen from his father's stash
soft circles in his wallet with some cash.
He wants to slip towards life through some locked portal,

not knowing what I know now, that his face
will never be more worth seeing. He thinks
he's less like Helen than Achilles, winks
at his jaunty unlit cigarette, blows

a kiss across two decades' emptiness —
how could he have guessed that sex was like pain,
too fleeting a glance at the gods' domain,
the hero's weeping over Patroclus

depicted in his textbook. That damn queer,
I can't forgive his innocence, as if
he might be just like anyone, his love
weak armies crushed in this heart lost to fear.

Piranhas

Discarded in a pond—some teenager's
black mood. Grown bored with watching it devour
hapless, shiny goldfish, he takes it there
one night, a thrumming plastic bag of water—
so desperate to escape. At the dark edge
he stoops, perhaps is sad a moment as
the thrashing suddenly goes silent, depth
is found. Ohio farmland menaces;
he's grateful when he sees the light of home,
the local strip mall's yellow double arch,
faint roar of traffic. Hungry and alone,
he microwaves some popcorn, takes the couch,
and clicks on Ozzy Osbourne's family.
They argue: sex, tattoos, what's on TV.

II.

Hispanic male, twenties, thin moustache,
around one-hundred sixty pounds, slicked back
black hair. "A predator," blares the newscast,
as next is flashed the little girl he took.
She looks like innocence, all that is lost
forever. Ravenous, we eat her up,
her soft white flesh and auburn curls—we must,
the story goes, have justice. Gaza strip,
twelve children dead as more Israeli bombs
hit terrorists; and on a lighter note,

a sixteen-inch piranha in a pond
was caught by anglers in Ohio. It did not
belong there — alien, a monster — how
it got there stumps officials in the town.

III.

I search for it in boxes in the basement.
Its demon visage haunts me, teeth exposed
by taxidermy's art. Such defacement,
I know now, but as a boy it seemed less posed.
A souvenir from hell — that awful trip
we took to see the Orinoco. Heat,
my parents arguing, mosquitoes, chirp
of tree frogs in the night — the river's might
seemed greater next to the small settlement.
There, *indios* sold tourists baskets, carved
trinkets, and *pirañas* — frozen regiments
on bamboo shelves. I cried, wanting to have
my specimen of rage — red belly, black fins,
those jaws that turned the weak to skeletons.

Brief Treatise on the New Millennial Poetics

Elizabeth Avenue, Elizabeth, New Jersey

Found rhythms: blast of gangsta rap, tires' screech,
the jangle just before a shop door slams.
The Polish-Portuguese *churrasquería*
escapes the poet's eye: to some, it is
unbeautiful, to others, merely quaint.
I notice in the empty lot next door
a makeshift baseball diamond, home to dreams
Dominican and Puerto Rican kids
still dream, though some of us hate sentiment,
while others only see the factories
that in the distance spew out wartime fumes.
The Catholic church greets worshipers, wide mouth
exhaling organ music, God's dank breath,
unsure if it's astonished or just bored.
My family's first years of exile here
were neither happiness nor weirdly fate:
necessity comes closer to the truth
of what Elizabeth, New Jersey meant
to us, hard winter streets heaped up with snow
that fell both magically and randomly,
a loveliness that terrified me. Now,
the tiny bakery that once gave warmth,
its glow like Cuba down the concrete block,
is utterly dilapidated. Smell
of bitter Cuban coffee, cigarettes —
a hint of guava, strangely sickly sweet.
What do the poets say? We must refuse
nostalgia's reassurance that the way

was clear; or else, observe the pastries glazed
like perfect porcelains, improbably
aligned. So orderly I must instead
confess I'm human, how they break my heart.

El Viejo y la Mar

My island, here I am addressing you
again. You're deaf as an old man, can't stand

straight anymore. We both should be ashamed
of this behavior — you, for your pride, me

for loving you with my womanly heart.
For once, won't you listen to what I say?

The winters here are very cold. I yearn
for your lean body next to mine, the night

remembering to keep its promises
to end, and to bring stars again. Your snore

growls like the jungle, your face is brown
from staring at the white sun. I've gone blind

hoping that you would die and leave me all
your riches — old man, what have you hidden

under the stone in the plaza? I thought
while I slept once, you rowed it out to sea

and cast it overboard, explaining the gold
that dances on the waves at sunset. You

old fool, all I can do is imagine
the humid warmth of your breezes, like rum's

hot perfume on your heavy, endless breath —
here I am, I've been waiting forever,

but you're drunk again on your own beauty,
while I still cry for punishing myself.

Ode to the Man Incidentally Caught in the Photograph of Us on My Desk

At first, you look determined, sunglasses
protecting your imaginary blue,
and therefore possibly sensitive, eyes.
You don't seem like the others, arms askew,
heads angled, asses in the air — you march
as if you think that life depended on
your mission. Out of focus, on the beach
we have our backs to, maybe it's forgone
to you, the heartening conclusion that
humanity must still be worth your care.
Around you teems the world at play, too fat,
too innocent, too broken to repair.
Much time has passed; the cheerful photograph
of us seems marred by your demeanor now,
as if the years of heedless frozen laughs
had changed your mind, as if you always knew
that any love was treacherous, that all
was somehow lost. Irretrievable friend,
your vaguely handsome face yet dutiful,
bear witness to us, even in the end.

The Enemy

The buildings' wounds are what I can't forget;
though nothing could absorb my sense of loss
I stared into their blackness, what was not

supposed to be there, billowing of soot
and ragged maw of splintered steel, glass.
The buildings' wounds are what I can't forget,

the people dropping past them, fleeting spots
approaching death as if concerned with grace.
I stared into the blackness, what was not

inhuman, since by men's hands they were wrought;
reflected on the TV's screen, my face
upon the buildings' wounds. I can't forget

this rage, I don't know what to do with it —
it's in my nightmares, towers, plumes of dust,
a staring in the blackness. What was not

conceivable is now our every thought:
We fear the enemy is all of us.
The buildings' wounds are what I can't forget.
I stared into their blackness, what was not.

God, Gays, and Guns

Inventing memories I've never had,
I think about the church that kept me safe,
kind neighbors who invited me to supper,
the garden where my grandparents grew squash.

But no — in church, I wasn't ever safe,
an outcast who just wanted to belong
in Eden, where desirous love was quashed.
I yearned for safety, wanted freedom more,

and wished that all the outcasts could belong.
My parents wanted me to love this place;
America, to them, was safe and free.
Its generosity still baffles me:

My parents taught me I should love, sow peace,
become a vessel of Christ's sacrifice.
His generosity still tortures me,
forgiving sins that seem like life's intention.

Become a vessel of Christ's sacrifice,
I give myself entirely to another
whose face forgives my sins and bad intentions.
Love for him — love for God and country —

could anyone give one up for another?
Go back, to that place of promise and loss,
love him still as you love God, in that country
that never existed, but someday might —

gone back to that place of the possible,
kind neighbors invite us now to supper,
we who exist to ask how we yet might
invent the memories I never had.

Patriotic Poem

after Neruda

The war on words had been declared. A voice
was now considered dangerous,
and could be confiscated by police.
A metaphor lay beaten in the street
while moonlight bathed it in white tears. The war
on words had been declared, in language none
could contradict. A lie ran naked through
the capital, while onlookers looked on.
It seemed that everything stopped making sense:
the punctuation of the traffic lights,
the thudding sound of dictionaries shut,
the heavy heart the poet wore to bed
for love. The war on words had been declared.
A lullaby defied the curfew, night
close in around it like swaddling clothes.
A girl spelled "moratorium" in school;
the next day she was dead, her hands sawn off
as punishment. The war on words had been
declared. Soon, silence stole over the land,
broken only by the piercing protest
of car alarms set off by no one's touch,
a neighbor's wailing weed-whacker, a song
that once remembered one cannot get out
of one's head. WAR ON WORDS DECLARED cried out
the evening paper, soundlessly, too late —
the President was on TV to say
we had won, we had won, we had won.

Post–9/11 Parable

It's almost March, the time when we —
(American democracy) —
might go to war against Iraq.

A nation injured in this way
cannot forgive its enemies.
It's almost March, the time when we

remember Jesus dying for
our sins. Good Christians, stoning whores,
demand a war against Iraq,

an eye for each unseeing eye,
tooth for decaying tooth. Winds rise:
it's almost March, the time when we

will bury spring's surprising dead.
Maimed children, mute counterattack,
won't stop this war against Iraq:

down from the mount, the F-16s
drop bombs, enough for all, exact.
It's almost March, the time when we
have gone to war against Iraq.

Sestina Dolorosa

The rain falls all day long, while I pursue
a memory of I'm not quite sure what.
A gray asthmatic tree begins to wheeze;
the wind picks up, dies down again, a slow,
relentless process. Thought resists, a mule
that won't pull any load. My desk lamp's light

encircles clutter: photos, bills past late,
as if they'd gathered specially to say
Don't write another word. Don't smile.
Outside, I'm sure of it, the street is wet,
a slick black tongue, always telling its lie.
Although I don't remember what it was,

I'm sure it had to do with distant wars.
The rain falls all day long; I hear the lilt
in water's quiet voice, the clouds slung low
as if to listen for its secrets. So
would I like listening, with snowmelt's weight,
in rivulets as truthful and as small

as those that run down window panes. I mull
decisions over in my mind. *Unwise,*
I think, *resist.* The fog grows densely white;
the chilly dampness almost seems half-lit.
Remembering I'm not sure what, I see
their broken bodies rotting where they lay,

rain falling on them, gently, constantly.
The mist borne by the wind can kill; the mills
along the river's edge make death. The sea
lumbers inland; three gulls have lost their ways
careening in this storm that will not lift.
Then, memory: fertile plains sown with wheat,

at last, the perfect gleam of dawn! We wait.
The sun rises graciously, almost sly,
strumming power lines like strings on a lute.
I know this country, recognize its miles
of kindness. *Whose is this land*, I ask, *whose?*
before a growl of thunder—it is she,

the all-pursuing rain, coat wet, soaked through.
I wake to this mess, no wars, yet; words lay
unworked in mills, unplayed upon their lute.

What Passes Now for Moral Discourse

O Lord, for whom we yet yearn, hear my prayer.
Here we are, before the moment of rapture.
The world, back-broken, awaits the last rupture —
When God looks away, appalled by the horrors
we each inflict upon the nameless other,
in the name of Christ, or Allah, whose grandeur
we diminish. We have become the creature
no deity would deign to call "child." Lovers
fear the body's speech, and the heart's sad labors
go on and on and on, each beat like torture.
The ends justify the means: time of terror,
time of vanquishing the Evil Empires,
of Great Communicators, private payers,
time of learning all we know from news features.
Here, now, the moment when we lose our future —
O Lord, whoever you are, hear my prayer.

from *Libro de Preguntas*

Si todos los ríos son dulces
de dónde saca sal el mar?

Cómo saben las estaciones
que deben cambiar de camisa?

Por qué tan lentas en invierno
y tan palpitantes después?

Y cómo saben las raíces
que deben subir a la luz?

Y luego saludar al aire
con tantas flores y colores?

Siempre es la misma primavera
la que repite su papel?

If sweet water flows in all the rivers,
from where does the ocean take its salt?

How do the seasons know
that they should change their costumes?

Why, so listless in winter,
are they so passionate after?

And how do the roots know
they should rise up toward the sun?

And later, wave at the air
with such flowers and colors?

Is it always the same Spring
who reprises her role, forever?

translated from the Spanish of Pablo Neruda

II. EIGHTEEN DAYS IN FRANCE

Eighteen Days in France

WHY WE NEVER TRAVEL

I've always wanted to return. Before
I learned the body's caves and slums,
I knew a sacred world my lover claims
lay not so far from here. It wasn't fear
that kept me — maybe it was something in
the river's murmuring, the sunset's peace
that did. The wounds of men are imprecise,
but even so, can kill. Inside their skin
I wandered, long vacations in their lungs,
my souvenirs a vertebra or tooth.
I lost my lover on a mountain path
above a waterfall that carved with song
its granite bed. I've always wanted to
go back, that bloodless peak, no heart as true.

MARILYN IN PARIS

Below the Place de la Sorbonne, we heard
them playing — bluesy jazz from a duet —
an old piano, and a clarinet.
A woman, housed in something like a shroud
of plastic bags, looked on with sadness,
and joy — the paradox is understood
in Paris, capital of the unfairly good.
It's later, when we wander along side-streets,
hands clasped for just a moment, that I wonder
exactly how that bruised piano landed there,
cramped sidewalk of a busy thoroughfare,
and why its tender music seemed an answer
to questions more keen. In her studio,
the master writes her poems: She would know.

OPEN AIR MARKET, LE MARAIS

Amidst his pyramids of golden ingots,
the man who sells foie gras seems very rich.
We sample some on squares of soft brioche
as pamphleteers alert us to the riots
that happened somewhere, in red headlines I
half-wish I understood. Too much to taste —
tart cherries from Provence, an olive paste,
some greens (arugula, to my surprise,
that looked to me like dandelion leaves).
The bitterness and sweetness mingle here
as easily as children play — her hair
in braids, a plump Eurasian girl contrives
pure joy from tossing coins to street musicians.
If only all the world schooled such magicians.

MAKING SENSE OF THE CURRENCY ON LINE
FOR LE MUSÉE PICASSO

However closer it might seem to art —
the brightly colored bills, the graceful figures
about to waltz off heavy coins — it pays for
the gasoline, the decaf and baguette.
To use a public toilet costs two francs,
a little less than what I give the man
without a leg whose sign I understand
(another universal language, inked
in French, called poverty and suffering) —
the smell of money, like the smell of piss,
is recognizable in any place.
For thirty francs, we're in: like broken things
too priceless to be thrown away, we see
Picassos everywhere, stark misery.

TACHYCARDIA AT THE CATHEDRAL OF NOTRE DAME

I'm here, but think of them, the ones I've left
for colleagues to console about the test
that's positive, the virus we detect
despite the triple cocktail, the shift
in white count signaling another — what?
I'm here, but think pneumonia, GC,
lymphoma, specters that will not recede
as easily as we re-think, forget —
I'm here, another country where I wish
there were no AIDS, and they are here with me,
my patients and my friends, their poetry
as yet unwritten, brows not feverish,
still here, with me, where I administer
just joy — pulses loudly beating, hearts stirred.

THE UNNAMED UNDERSTOOD

All day, we searched for it, the restaurant
that Marilyn had claimed served only boar.
We didn't know what we were looking for
as through each sun-worn village we would squint
at homely storefronts with their tilted signs
that usually announced "FERMÉ." A taste
for game (intensified by all the craze
about "mad cow" — though each we passed seemed sane,
bovinely calm, behind its barbed-wire fence)
had led to our obsessed pursuit. We found
a likely candidate, but like its town,
it was completely boarded up — in French,
spray-painted reasons we could not decipher,
as if tattooed on it names of dead lovers.

DETOUR

Why is it that this verdant countryside
reminds me of their bodies? Muscular
like Gary, or Tyrell, the way they were —
in almost casual repose, pre-AIDS.
We're getting lost among the vineyards now,
impressed by the occasional chateau,
each one a grandiose yet heartfelt vow
against surrender. Why did I not know
enough to save them? Birds fly low, as if
reluctant to be parted from forbidden
earthly consorts; the entire world seems hidden,
for just a moment, by some passing wisps
of cloud. The stolen sun, returned to us,
is harrowing as it is glorious.

POSTCARD FROM BURGUNDY

Dear Marilyn,
　　　　　We've made it to Bouilland!
There's almost nothing here — we hiked last night
along a hillside road which at its height
was crowned with firs and poplars joined in stands,
last pilgrims to a solemn, ruined abbey.
I thought of you as we ascended, breath
as urgent as the hunger of your grief.
Above the broken transept's arches, happy
birds dipped and soared. The moon was rising fast,
to cast its eeriness around the place;
the columbines beneath the Queen-Anne's-lace
seemed each a tragicomic jester's face
that jeered but pitied us on our return,
taught something I'm not sure is ever learned.

SUMMER VACATION READING

Leaving the inn, we step out into sun
so bright I flash back to the white ER:
surrounding vineyards neat as cornrowed hair,
exposed earth black as her deflated skin.
I almost yearn for that lost urgency,
when briefly doctors treated love as a scourge,
French novels giving way to French research,
sad Madame Bovary to HIV.
When I touched her bony arm, it was not
impossible that she would die. In fact,
she did, blood poisoned by our bumbling acts
as much as by what seemed the opposite
of this complacency. Her silent stare
still burns as she refuses our best care.

HOSPICES DE BEAUNE, HÔTEL-DIEU

How little we've advanced in medicine:
beneath the fifteenth-century stained glass
their gruesome transphrenations let release
the noxious humors they thought caused by sin
as much as by disease. The images
and instruments that they preserved recall
our human needs, for doing good as well
as punishing the awful godlessness
that agony is sometimes taken for.
Saint Michael weighed their souls, his placid face
of little comfort as they died; Christ's grace
remains elusive, as so many more
of us are damned than saved. The sisters prayed,
as I do, now — mistrustful, still afraid.

THE OLIVE GROVE

How many centuries ago these trees
were planted is unknown, but some have guessed
the Romans planned these hilltop terraces.
The scowling faces in the bark agree
on nothing in their silent arguments,
except that they'll bear fruit again, green globes
hard with their bitterness. The sunset glows
and sends long shadows stretching through their midst,
akin to how I yearn for you — how old
is need, how tangled up in ancient knots.
You've wandered off from me, drawn by the scents
of lavender and jasmine on the cold
breeze rising up from where a garden pleads:
the olive grove's grudged shelter seems betrayed.

ABOVE AGUY

A rock-strewn, reddish landscape — foreign land,
but not so alien as Mars — spread out
before us, radiating waves of heat.
The guidebook promised panoramas, grand
and almost limitless — slight carsickness
from driving on the winding coastal roads
disoriented us enough to lead
me to proclaim I'd sighted Africa's
lush shores. The sea was frighteningly blue;
the tiny town below us knelt to it,
as if in awe of beauty's absolute,
remorseless power over humble truth.
This planet of our petty human wars,
how lost we seemed, impossible and sure.

ROMAN FRÉJUS

Decaying columns overgrown with weeds
are all that's really here, the skeleton
of some vast beast left bleaching in the sun
that makes us wonder how it died. Faint words
in Latin dedicate a toppled arch;
small bits of colored rock in a mosaic
depict a noblewoman's painted, stoic,
compliant lips. Too easily, we search
for something we might reconstruct as us:
Did two men ever walk what seems to be
a road beside the baths as quietly
as we do now, in love? Ridiculous —
and yet to know that neither will we last
is why we've come, enamored of the past.

POSTCARD FROM MONACO

Dear M.,

      We're here, where countries' borders seem
so trivial. We simply drove right in,
no passports necessary, no long line
to have your suitcase searched. It's like a dream,
this kind of freedom, even if it does
seemed purchased by the filthy rich. Rolls-Royce,
Ferrari, Porsche — is luxury the price
one has to pay to live in paradise?
(The gated villas make the cars look cheap.)
I've wondered what it's possible to own —
right now, I'd give it all away to know
J.'s joy as he picks his way down the beach
to steal a dip in this ownerless sea.
We send our love — he is in to his knees!

FOUND AMONG DISCARDED PHOTOGRAPHS

We were there, however briefly. What changed?
The place itself cannot remember us —
the blackbirds that seemed caged inside the ribs
of pines dispersed upon the church bell's clang.
But we were there, remarking on the beauty of
the town's small square, the anonymity
of shops and restaurants, and balconies
whose red bougainvillea flung themselves off,
ruined by unrequited love. We've changed
since we were there, and what we can recall —
the injury of red blooms on white walls,
the unfelt emptying of startled wings —
is nothing but God's punishment for all
we have forgotten in ourselves to praise,
for all such wonders truth could not reprise.

REST STOP NEAR THE ITALIAN BORDER

Alps crowding in the distance, gas tank low,
we stop beneath the diesel clouds of trucks —
black radiators, ugly stars of bugs
squashed flat. You say you need to go.
A Muslim family, Algerian
perhaps, drifts by, the woman's robes
bright fluttering amidst the roar the road's
unending traffic raises. Evian,
some candy to defuse my garlic breath —
you're off, determined, and so I'm left
with just the warmth of your hand's soft,
negligible weight. A hand I held, near death,
back home — I can't recall his name,
but speeding, inescapable, was what came.

POSTCARD MAILED FROM THE AIRPORT

Dear M.,

       I'm writing now from CDG.
It seems impossible we're going home —
so much we haven't seen. Next year, to Rome?
By then, all this will be a memory.
And yet, I know it's changed me, being here
on this old earth. They're here, you know, my patients,
the ones who died on me too young — their passions,
their laughter and first tastes of caviar,
their spindly arms that reach out towards the sun
amidst the plane trees and the monuments.
They talked to me from deep in catacombs;
they smelled like grass, in parks rinsed clean by rain.
So many parks in Paris — in warm bread
broken, their steaming breath — last mornings, shared.

THE RETURN

after Mary Campbell's Wonder and Science

I think I took too much Imodium,
for fear the gastroenteritis I'd
come down with would make miserable the flight.
My mind went feverishly, blindly numb;
I couldn't think of France at all, as though
it were a weird invented netherworld,
a place as narrow as it must be wide,
where savages unthinkably uncouth
resided amidst hoards of precious gold.
I knew I'd traveled across endless seas
to reach its fabled shores, so endlessly
it seemed as though the sciences I loved
were still evolving, and that I, explorer
and God's brave soldier, might there dwell forever.

III. TOWARD A THEORY OF MEMORY

from *Cien Sonetos de Amor*

XLIV

Sabrás que no te amo y que te amo
puesto que de dos modos es la vida,
la palabra es un ala del silencio,
el fuego tiene una mitad de frío.

Yo te amo para comenzar a amarte,
para recomenzar el infinito
y para no dejar de amarte nunca:
por eso no te amo todavía.

Te amo y no te amo como si tuviera
en mis manos las llaves de la dicha
y un incierto destino desdichado.

Mi amor tiene dos vidas para amarte.
Por eso te amo cuando no te amo
y por eso te amo cuando te amo.

XLIV

You will know that I do and do not love you
just as life is of two minds,
a word is one wing of silence,
and fire is half made of ice.

I love you just so I can begin to love you,
to begin anew at the infinite
and to be able never to stop loving you:
For these reasons, I do not love you yet.

I do and do not love you as if I held
in my hands the keys to every happiness
and an uncertain, unhappy fate.

My love has two lifetimes to love you.
That's how I can love you when I don't,
and still love you when I do.

LXVI

No te quiero sino porque te quiero
y de quererte a no quererte llego
y de esperarte cuando no te espero
pasa mi corazón del frío al fuego.

Te quiero sólo porque a ti te quiero,
te odio sin fin, y odiándote te ruego,
y la medida de mi amor viajero
es no verte y amarte como un ciego.

Tal vez consumirá la luz de enero,
su rayo cruel, mi corazón entero,
robándome la llave del sosiego.

En esta historia sólo yo me muero
y moriré de amor porque te quiero,
porque te quiero, amor, a sangre y fuego.

LXVI

I don't love you only because I love you
and from loving you I start not loving you,
and yet from waiting for you when I don't expect you
my cold heart begins to burn for you.

I love you only because it is you I love,
I hate you endlessly, and in hating you I beg you,
and it's the measure of my vagrant love
not to see you and yet to love you blindly too.

Maybe January's light will consume
my entire heart in its cruel rays,
robbing me of my key to the quiet sublime.

In this story, only I die today,
and I will die of love because I love you,
because I love you, my love, mercilessly, crazed.

XCIV

Si muero, sobrevíveme con tanta fuerza pura
que despiertes la furia del pálido y del frío,
de sur a sur levanta tus ojos indelebles,
de sol a sol que suene tu boca de guitarra.

No quiero que vacilen tu risa ni tus pasos,
no quiero que se muera mi herencia de alegría,
no llames a mi pecho, estoy ausente.
Vive en mi ausencia como en una casa.

Es una casa tan grande la ausencia
que pasarás en ella a través de los muros
y colgarás los cuadros en el aire.

Es una casa tan transparente la ausencia
que yo sin vida te veré vivir
y si sufres, mi amor, me moriré otra vez.

XCIV

Should I die, survive me with a force so pure
that you awaken fury from the pale, chill world,
in all directions raise your indelible eyes,
day in, day out, sound your mouth's guitar.

I don't want your footsteps to vacillate
nor your smile wane, I don't want my bequeathed joy
to die. Don't come knocking at my chest, I'm away.
Dwell in my absence as you would in my estate.

Absence is such a vast house
that you will walk through its walls
and hang paintings in the air.

Absence is such a transparent house
that without my own life I will watch you live
and if I see you suffer, my love, I will die again.

A Simple Cuban Meal

We gather at the table, even those
who left us long ago. We eat roast pork,
black beans and rice, and tell the story of
the avocado tree that had to be
cut down, that took so many years to bear—
but once it did, how generous it was!
I see Abuela halving one, sharp knife
through soft green flesh; she'd gather them beneath
a shade so dense I thought it permanent.
A freak windstorm felled it. It listed like
a sinking ship a week or two before
the man came with his chainsaw. "Memories,"
she'd shrug, when I spoke wistfully of it.
She never seemed to miss that tree, although
it was a few more years after she died
before we'd have an avocado in
a salad. Tasting it, I understand
how little pleasure teaches us in life.
Much more honorable is sacrifice.

The Sailfish

Like some shivering joy, some piercing hope,
how high you must have lunged. She landed you,
but not the future that she'd dreamed. Their few
years shared together captured in your shape —

the shining arc your body is, upslope
of your fine bill, great dorsal fin as blue
as some shimmering joy, some spreading hope.
You must have lunged before she landed you,

his arms steadying hers as you dove deep,
the urgency of his embrace made new
by fear of losing the beauty they knew
you'd be. Swim this wall now and never stop,
like some sorrowing joy, some sounding hope.

Ganymede, to Zeus

High priest, friend's father, basketball
coach — watch, you seize me by the pool,

behind the library, or in
the bottom bunk while a strange wind

spins fish in an aquarium.
Your clutch upon my pallid skin

is like the scratched calligraphy
you teach me — watch, see my slapped cheek,

apple for the teacher, white meat
or dark in the camp's mess hall. Eat

these memories with me, *this bread*
His body, blood of Christ our Lord

amen. Among the Eagle scouts
always one, gold talons flared out

grasp at his own lost beautiful
soul. Kisses that disembowel,

eyes that penetrate — eyes I feel
as we rise up toward the defiled

yet still glorious sun. The world
does not die for me; instead, turned

from me, like your face gone blank,
it scathes me in its secret stink.

You call. I bring your coffee cup,
your sweat-streaked shirt, your baseball cap—

I was eight. Father, swimming coach,
crossing guard. Naked for you. Watch.

After the Long Drive

Night. Pine trees gathering along the road
like spectators cheering a race's end,
made ghostly by the headlights' glare, a blur.
At intervals, the service stations glow,
bright promises of sustenance; they seem
to fade by more reluctantly, afraid
as we are of the possibilities
of solitude. We've made this trip before.

Paint splattered on the exit sign for Sandwich
is cause for feeling wounded: perfect aim
of highway lane divider, spears of white
that pierce me silently, unendingly.
The riot of another person's trash
dumped on the median enrages me.
The love song mewling on the radio
is all you've never said to me before.

I wake from having drifted off, and this
is what I dreamed. A question mark of twine
is caught up in the dancing seagrass. Light.
It's like America, but in a time of peace.
AIDS, terrorism, Red Sox games discussed
while you make perfect sandwiches for guests.
A pine tree shines with Christmas ornaments.
You smile at me, you love me like before.

The town is changing: fewer Portuguese,
the artists almost gone. Rain begins to fall,
all dreariness and jewels at once. Two men
speed up their pace, hands clasped as suddenly
they skip across the street. A memory
intrudes on me, the joy I felt when once
we dreamed together what we'd never known —
before I knew there'd ever be "before."

For Jorge, after Twenty Years

What might I say to you that now would seem
like something new? I spent my day entranced
by sounds the cooling rain made, watching steam

rise lazily from asphalt; once, you danced
in rain like this to make me laugh, that summer
we spent in Oxford, teenagers who sensed

in early friendship more than jest, a stronger
beating of hearts when you pulled off your shirt,
oblivious to faintly British twitter

your muscled chest elicited from "birds"
(we'd learned to call them that) in uniforms —
blue boyish blazers over prim plaid skirts —

streaked hair and freckled noses we would scorn.
That cobblestone side street led years ago
to a smallish room not really in a dorm

(its walls were curved and three feet thick) aglow
with lamplight. Unromantically, we kissed,
the first time I felt terror: we were gay,

I knew it long before, but unexpressed
at such proximity (I still can see
your face, so close its pores grew bottomless)

it seemed more safely possibility.
Not so from that point forward. Credible,
the August clouds cast doubt on novelty;

I couldn't hold your hand, the Cock and Bull
as threatening as the mute library.
I wonder now if you believe it will

be better someday, like the memory
I have of us back then, when we would hope
in conversations half-forgotten over tea

(outside the steamed-up window, while it steeped,
the pigeons bowing courteously to mates)
that how we felt — scared, loved — would never stop.

It's twenty years since then, or since we met —
the anniversaries have long been blurred.
First kiss, first time we fucked, first sacrament

(communion at my brother's wedding) shared.
We tolerate each other's absences
much better than we used to. Unprepared,

I'll venture in the rain alone and wish
I had a good umbrella, or the flash
of your young restless body, or your voice

that tells me not what I forgot, but laughs.
You're at a conference in Chicago; I'm
away in Montréal next week. Our paths

are taking us away from fear; in time,
perhaps we'll trust this love enough to leave
each other decently, shouldering what tamed

that awful passion privately, as grief
is borne. When I return, soaked through, I'll heat
the chicken curry in the microwave,

the leftovers of what we had last week
when you surprised me by remembering
an Indian restaurant where we'd eat

(ten blocks away, the count by church bells' clang)
if in the dining hall was kidney pie.
"It doesn't taste the same," you said — the sting

of clove and pepper brought tears to our eyes.
That night, we made love as we often do,
more quietly than with abandon's cries.
You smiled slightly; I thought I knew why.

Song in the Off-Season

Last boats point windward in the harbor.
The clanging buoys mark their shoals,
as if the sea were time, its danger, hours.
The restaurants are shuttered closed.

October: doddering leaves tell
the same old stories to the wind.
The secret reasons for their fall
remain unsaid, to our chagrin.

Off-season, those who still remain
look hungry, like they want to know.
The older couple, gripped in pain;
the stray white cat, portent of snow.

You're here with me, near the world's end.
A cup of tea pretends to dream;
we read. It's good to be back in.
Let the night come, the lamp gleam:

We're sure of insecurity.
Floors creak, from no one's weight but home's.
My love, you asked what we should be.
It's not enough, what we've become?

Catastrophic Sestina

I remember the terrible blizzard
of '78. All night long, the darkness danced
with what turned out to be a blinding day. You
brewed coffee bravely while the thunder rumbled.
From the dorm's window, I couldn't see the street signs
while furiously I was doing my assignment

for Biochemistry. You were doing the assistant
from Thermodynamics lab, maker of volcanic eruptions
that reeked of sulfur and chlorine. It was a sign,
you said; a few days later, after we danced
at some strobe-lit, raging frat party, you mumbled
something like "I've wanted to fuck you

since the beginning of time." I remember undressing you;
at that moment, I was doing anything but
thinking, so close I could hear your stomach grumble.
My tears the next morning came in a flood.
Our clothes, entangled near the bed, danced
as if still drunk. Outside, the world full of signs

and portents: even the melting snow was a sign,
impermanence, impermanence. I looked at you,
trying so hard to make my stilled heart dance
again. You looked like you were daydreaming about
a natural disaster in some far-off land, an earthquake
that could make the whole lost planet crumble.

In my heart, I knew you were right. I trembled
as I ran my hand through your hair, its designs
and swirls colliding galaxies, tiny black tsunamis,
dooming me to be swallowed forever in you,
just another casualty, barely enduring recent events.
Last chance, I remember thinking, *last dance*,

last chance, last dance for love — that to dance
was to break open life, to make the frail body resemble
that utter disintegration we fear. Drawing an ashen portrait
on the canvas of white sheets, I resigned
myself to save what I could, to love my own destruction in you.
Quiet as an avalanche, sudden as a landslide

I was dying of astonishment. No one danced
to ward off the tornados, whose distant rumble
I took for a sign. I remember wanting only to protect you.

Toward a Theory of Memory

You can never go back. Roaring past stands
of exhaust-stunted pines, we carry too much
with us, to where so many years ago
we met in each the other —

already half our lives gone by? — beginning then
what has since become this long accumulation,
this effort to make knowable a history,
as if the duffle bag,

the battered journal, the sunglasses once lost
and then after a days-long search regained,
the unconsciously memorized sequence
of highway exits,

the Doberman made almost small by napping
in a knot on the back seat, as if each
were purposefully adding up
to something certain.

And there it is, exactly as we left it,
although perhaps the drive from the toll booths
to the stately red brick buildings, home
to other students now,

seems shorter, or at least less promising,
less an opening to the universe.
Here is where we learned how time changes us,
first inklings of truth's

relentless and impossible defining,
the parsec in freshman astronomy
at once exact and stretching out a distance
I could not imagine,

as far as I could travel reading Coleridge
and Dickinson beneath the quad's great oaks,
a place both recognizable and not.
I suppose that's why

we want so much to return, wondering
if still that spot exists, and knowing it
cannot. You point out new construction,
a student center

sprawling out upon what was a favorite expanse
of lawn, traversed so many times each spring,
the earth's warm breath upon our pumping legs,
rushing to get there,

down the hill, past the ugly "social dorms"
beyond which railroad tracks divided
the campus from what might best be called a meadow
dotted with birches,

some old enough to have unraveling bark,
dissolution that seemed mysterious
beneath such young green leaves that gave us shade.
We park the suv

and from the opened back hatch out bounds Ruby;
you pull the comforter from the duffle bag,
while I collect the cooler (peanut butter
on whole wheat, carrot sticks,

two cold, clear bottles of Poland Spring) and
the books we're working on, like coursework we assign
ourselves, habit of our education here.
I remember when

weeks back you flushed me out of bed to see
the first open blossom on the hyacinths
you forced, so proud of your discovery
that something new could be

coaxed up from winter's usual nothingness,
its expected, dependable devolution,
and how in that tiny pink cup it seemed
the world might be contained,

that in it I could descend deeper and deeper
until I was able again to trust anything,
to pretend that one can yet revert to innocence.
I feel a slight pain now

as we come upon the tall, familiar grass,
insects set skittering by our footsteps
then alighting who knows where but in
a line I'll scribble down

possessing nothing of them except dust,
a rusting oil drum at one far corner red-brown
as cinnamon, the birches, perhaps more stout,
bent forward as if they'd

prepared their bower specially for us. You spread
the comforter, leave two decades' same half for me
to lay beside you. Birds sing their songs of need,
communicating

hunger, alarm, sexual deeds; it is all
still here, if not exactly as it once was, then
the way we might want it, having been there
once and come, gladly, again.

Patagonia

Atop the glacier, peering into rooms
inhabited by past millennia's
immense yet utterly silent blue ghosts,
how hard, how very pure I thought my love
might be, if entering eternity
only were possible. Instead, we crunched
along, the sun and so much chilly air
and the short distance between us so bright
I knew my pounding heart was temporary,
my breathlessness another language for
the insignificance of my desire,
the vastness of our hope for something more.

Defense of Marriage

May 16, 2004

Will you remember me the way I am
today? This long engagement — twenty years —
has taken something of a toll. I came
to bed last night, and thought that we were far

from being done with dreams. You turned to me,
and I was young, and still afraid; June's moon
peered in, parental with concern. My knee
ached, punishment for worshipping the loam

in our small garden. Irises in bloom,
their wizened, bearded faces beautiful
old men's, dispensed their blessings and their blame.
You painted furniture, and said "I will,

of course I will." I planted savory,
not hardy through the winter months, beside
the mint you hate for its invasiveness.
A breeze intruded, always the bright bride

the whole world wants to marry. A life's work,
as yet only half-done, ubiquitous —
I felt tired, and it would soon be dark,
but none can refuse love, not even us.

The Story of Us

Its spangled blanket spread out on the waves,
the afternoon seems here with us, concerned
with nothing but what must be called one life.
Nowhere is it clearer than in Provincetown.
The beach arcs outward in the distance, poised
as if it might embrace us all in its
great sandy arms; like raucous seraphim
the gulls dip down, bestowing blessings on
the kids who toss them halves of pretzel sticks
then eat the other halves themselves. Retired
gay men read *Glamour*, their umbrellas' shade
bedecked in tapestries Scheherazade
might well have rested on from desert heat.
A toddler stammers with the effort in
her narrative, first act of human noise;
a young girl stares at someone with desire.
Last night, I heard a poet read; his word-play
made tears spring from my eyes. It felt so strange,
at first, to be so touched, as from within —
as though I'd touched myself, stroked my own skin.
He said that all art couldn't help but fail —
that all we can create is allegory
while truth, like last night's starry, blue-black sky,
eludes us. So I stared at them, their twinkling trail
across the vast expanse above at once
impossible and yet perceptible,
his voice still ringing through me, asking why
and answering: he spoke both artfully and still
so purely paradox made perfect sense.

I walked home through the prism of houselights—
echoed laughter, clatter of silverware
returned to kitchen drawers—I was one
with something called a neighborhood, a place.
It's evening now; gulls cry in notes that range
from joy to melancholy. In your face,
a light that I'd call "empathy," aware
of how the term constructs what's just emotion—
but as the poet said, I realize,
it's in another person's heart, his eyes,
that the story of us achieves completion.

The Sodomite's Lament

Why was he punished? Hell if I know. Yes,
we were lovers, as if in Sodom this

were something anyone would be ashamed
of! Lot, poor pious Lot—I say his name

and still I hate him for his cowardice.
He promised me his love, a paradise

of morning birdsong, safe from common thieves,
a place beyond this desert's stifling grief.

I'm fortunate I left him when I did:
They say it was God's wrath, that he destroyed

the cities for their pride and sinfulness.
I say it was something else, selfishness

maybe, this God incapable of love
himself: Heard what he did to Lot's shamed wife?

He never said her name to me, but salt
enriches tears so all may taste her faults,

blown into our eyes by the searing wind.
Dumb woman, to think she was different—

we keep nothing in this world, not the trees,
not love, not even our own memories.

Equinoctial Downpour

We stood beneath the maples and the oaks
as if in rooms laid waste by flood, wet leaves
in golds and oranges and speckled reds
like irreplaceable possessions lost
forever. Brownstones sorrowed quietly
across the street, their countenances old
and knowing, having watched for years
the park and its small tragedies. The man
who led the murmuring gray pigeons down
the mall was once a politician, long
gone mad; occasional stray cats found dead
by children playing under bushes; none
to lay a wreath at the memorial
for Boston's heroes killed in World War I.
The boundary keeping present from the past,
like fog's uncertain touch, falls indistinct.
We stand here, waiting for the rain's return,
the neighbors we don't know who hurry past
not realizing what has ruined us
is gone, and yet is come to us again.

Pantoum for Our Imagined Break-Up

I can't imagine breaking up with you.
Instead, I think about the neighbors' problems:
His anguished look seems punishment for truth;
his "other half" is thin and Puerto Rican.

I think I know about the neighbors' problems.
They argue over nothing: TV sitcoms,
half-and-half or skim, trips to Puerto Rico.
I try to picture them undressing, fucking.

We argue over some new TV sitcom;
it's nothing, but I'm crying afterwards.
Later, you undress me; then you fuck me
rather than apologize. "I love you" — hard,

you say it like it's nothing. Cries, hard words
that drift across our shared side yard, they fight.
So I apologize, say, "I love you, George."
I don't know why it has to be this way.

Leaves drift across our shared side yard; cats fight,
their anguish somehow punishing and true,
I don't know why. It has to be this way,
I can't imagine breaking up with you.

The Changing of the Seasons

1. Spring: The Public Gardens

The yellow taxi of forsythia
appears, to speed us on to longer days.

2. Summer: Jamaica Pond

Four swans glide past, ignoring rusted signs
that warn ICE SKATING STRICTLY PROHIBITED.

3. Autumn: Marlborough Street

In burnished wood of the lit entryway
he bathed, as if in a snifter of cognac.

4. Winter: Logan International Airport

Snow swirling upwards outside, huge black windows:
My love, we have grown galaxies apart.

Once, It Seemed Better

Rain all day, but it doesn't matter:
I'm home alone. You left your presence,
though. Here in my study, it's sadder

for having to observe the ladder
that looms, like unrealized promise,
beneath the leaky skylight. Matters

as yet unattended to chatter
in your unmistakable cadence;
I'm not sure which of them seems sadder,

the deflated figure in the clutter
of your pulled-off clothes, or the romance
of your cup and spoon. What most matters

to me now, despite the soft shudder
(as if a place could have a conscience)
the whole house gives, is even sadder,

even colder: your absence, bitter
as it seems, invites forbearance.
Rain all day, and it hardly matters.
Here, without you, I wish I were sadder.

October, Last Sail

Among the last boats in the harbor, ours
seems glad for human company: you board,
and *El Poeta* rocks you lovingly.
I watch you from the pebbled beach, unsure.
But soon enough we're sailing out, the day
unpromising and cold; the air is gray,
the sun a milky yellow pearl inside
an oyster's opalescent shell. We round
the great curved sandy point, the open sea
monotonously green, while back on shore
the distant oranges and browns explain
the ancients' understanding of the earth's
emotions: anger mixed with mourning, loss
so vast that only god could suffer it.
I look to you for comfort, but your eyes
prefer how the horizon never ends.

Dawn, New Age

Neanderthal, giant rat, dinosaur:
forsaken creatures from your repertoire.
What made them less than perfect for this world?
Did you encode that they should not survive?

Forsaken creatures from your repertoire
arranged in sterile cases conjure you.
Did you encode this wish that we'd survive?
Their bones look strong from outside looking in

arranged in sterile cases, doubting you.
Progression of skulls: you make room for you.
Their bones look strong from outside looking in,
but what they lacked was wonder that they lived.

Progression of skulls, and soon we'll make you
serve our needs, cures for cancer, cures for AIDS,
the wonders that we lack to help us live.
Theories on your selfishness go extinct.

Serve our needs: after cancer, cure old age.
Our selfishness will make us go extinct
as wonder is consumed to help us live,
Neanderthals, giant rats, dinosaurs.

Allegorical

In the beginning, time was animal.
Instead of clocks, cocks announced the sunrise.
The night went on and on, in the dark cries
of wolves, who lapped up truth from moonlit pools.
It took forever for the vole to lose
its sight while it was hiding underground
(and so we think of sight as less than sound).
The ages of the muddy, muscled moose
were shown by its great height: tall centuries
surveyed the marshes that the glaciers made.
It fell to us, ingenious as toads,
to ask why we must wait so patiently.
By the seventh day, we had learned to count,
when all creation knew peace had run out.

Progress

Once,
       what we most feared was the utter loss
of everything, as with the terrible flash
of nuclear annihilation — Dad
exhausted, leaving anyway to go
to night school, and never coming back
before the permanent and scathing dawn.

Then,

technology began to seem more quaint,
(the cuteness of cloned lambs, adorable
septuplets, galaxies as finely wrought
as grandmother's lace handkerchiefs), so what
we feared was something more like having far
too much — my mother's recipe for sauce
perfected by immortalized tomatoes, red
like no tomorrow, red beyond belief.

Now,

it's here, the chance we only dreamed we'd have.
We fear nothing but each other, a fear
much easier to fathom. Flay a Jew
long distance, stone a Muslim in your heart.
The terrorist with small pox in a jar
is only a reminder of a quest
for which we've grown nostalgic, when the dead
spoke stupidly, providing comfort. Here,
in the land of the invincible, all
is certain, undeniable, at last.

The Crocuses

The crocuses keep coming up, though they
are dying. Made more beautiful, I think,
by sunlight passing through their petals: white,
purple, yellow, lavender. Memory
is like this, dependable as a rite.
And so I see my mother tending hers,
bright spring of her unhappy youth; they wink
at us with every chilling breeze. And so
I see us planting these, how gently you
delivered each small bulb to its dark hole,
so carefully it made me love you more.
And so it's come to this, the play of light
through colors I remember, helped create,
and know will only last a week or two,
harbingers of what's never seemed new life.
The crocuses will be gone soon enough.

Crybaby Haiku

1.

Downed white petals feign
shattered ice. Dead orchards wait
to grow whole again.

2.

Poetry like shit
floats fragmented on such thin
waters of delight.

3.

Many John Deere cranes
rooting in an asphalt pit.
They flail in the rain.

4.

Another day lit
from behind clouds. Great gray brain,
sky turned sentient.

5.

Patience for this wanes:
break the line at "tolerate,"
force a rhyme, with "sane."

6.

What can we know but
smallest pieces, tiny grains
of truth? Just all that.

7.

Here is my refrain.
Art never gets it quite right.
Here is my refrain.

8.

And so I repeat
the same damn mistake I strain
to avoid, forget.

9.

Seventeen less nine
always equals (roughly) eight.
Counting is in vain.

10.

What I can't invent
I try instead to retrain —
narrative in ruts.

11.

Five Marines slain
today, bodies blown to bits.
We think we know pain.

12.

Like shoes that don't fit,
form seems ever more arcane.
Writing hurts my feet.

13.

Who lives down the lane?
The little boy with hands cut
off. He has no name.

14.

Leaving something out
(guess at what I really mean)
is needed to write.

15.

Dear You, I Remain
Your Servant, Obedient,
angry and profane.

16.

Almost time to quit.
I consider what I've gained,
sucking cigarettes.

17.

Verbal legerdemain
is enough to get me hot.
Haven't I explained?

"SILENCE = DEATH"

His worn-out T-shirt, black as mourning, black
as countless deaths, surprises me — it screams
a phrase I've heard so many countless times
before, in words hot pink as countless
fevers — heat of language, demonstrations,
why does it still threaten me, I who held
my patient's hand who died his wordless death,
the respirator hissing in my ear
the countless breaths he couldn't take himself.
That was years ago, almost decades now.
Today, I see his T-shirt and I think
he isn't taking all his antiviral meds,
the countless pills he piled on my desk
to silence me, my T-cell counts and viral loads
detectable at greater than one hundred thousand,
the silent viral particles that swell
to numbers more than even we will count —
I pause, and shift a moment in my chair;
I ask, "How many loved ones did you lose?"
"I can't count them" is his response. "But one
left me this stupid T-shirt when he died."
Then, we're silent, counting moments, death
counting us in all its infiniteness,
in all we know that words will not explain.

Clinical Vignettes

1. HIV

I'm sure I got it on that trip
to Washington. In a men's room
at Reagan National. My name
as he said it kept echoing
across the hospital-white tiles
again, again, like history,
like something maybe we'd forget.
I've never felt ashamed of it.

2. Diabetes

That time I was accosted back
in Louisville — don't let 'em tell
you black folks say they safe there! — my blood
in my own smashed mouth tasted sweet,
my busted teeth was like hard candies.
I knew I had it, didn't need
no damn white doctor telling me
he knew my insides better'n me.

3. Breast Cancer

Before he found the lump, I thought
I can't believe I let him touch
my breast — I thought *a stranger's need* —
and that was when he stopped and frowned.
Before he said a word, I knew
that I had cancer, touching me
that way, that rough unfeeling hand
at once my crime and punishment.

4. Depression

Dog's high-pitched whine: Impossible
to translate, yet exactly how
it feels. Don't speak; the injury
may not have even happened yet.
The tap of slippers in the night
the sleepless story that I try
to type, the laptop's glow like hope.
Senseless tears, while elsewhere bombs drop.

You Bring Out the Doctor in Me

after Sandra Cisneros

You bring out the doctor in me
The smart perfume of antiseptics
The possibly unsound heart through the stethoscope
The naked under this paper drape in me.

You bring out the this won't hurt a bit in me
The scrubs that look like pajamas
The crude anatomical diagrams
The skin is the largest organ in me.

I'd let you draw my blood
The sting of my own needles,
The cold metal of fact in me.
Test it for secret love, for HIV.
I'd die for you, to have you in me.
Just you. No latex.
Just you and me.

You bring out the health care proxy in me.
Do not resuscitate
Do not intubate me.
You bring out the chaplain praying in me.
The IV bag hanging, glassy fluids in me.
The nurse in white sneakers toileting me.
The morphine drip, the dream of you dreaming me.
Maybe I'm dying. Maybe.

You bring out the helplessness in me
The limits of knowledge in me
The inability to cry in me.
You bring out the doctor in me.
You can't cure me: adore me.
Let me show you. Love
The only way I know how.

Composite of Three Poems from the Same Anthology by Williams, Rukeyser, and Sexton

I.

Once, there was no time. Instead,
what we now call Queen-Anne's-lace
stretched out around here endlessly.
Tiny purple hearts we wanted to possess.

II.

Later, in the dark time of Icarus,
we'd learned enough to question
ingenuity. Left behind, a woman's voice over waves
grieved insistently, but she did not cry.

III.

Now, we have survived the modern dream.
An airplane crashes, we watch funerals on TV;
my mother tells my father that she gave up art
for him, painting huge red tulips in the basement.

IV.

Once, I wished I were a woman.
I tried to kill myself, but couldn't.
I could write about it now, but screw it —
tomorrow, we might realize the human.

Tuesday Morning

The world awakening again, great stretch
of sky, its limbs the pinkish cirrus clouds
that lift away. But how to bless the day
already crowded with the sounds of trucks
downshifting, laden with their cargo, blare

of morning headlines while my love works out,
the neighbors' barking mutts. It's all been said
before, and even the embarrassment
of my erection makes no novel point:
What need is there for pleasure, when today

I'll diagnose a man with cancer, not
know what to say. Believing in the poem
provides not much relief. I hear the grief
in a descending airplane's roar, arrived
from Buenos Aires or from Amsterdam—

the clouds embrace the disappearing moon,
but even this transparent metaphor
offers little comfort. No poet cares
for such deceptions anymore, and words
don't cure. The sky continues brightening

but irony is lost on me forever.
Who wants religion, who would ask forgiveness?
Car door slams; momentary angled light
sweeps through our half-dark bedroom like the flight
of some enormous, awkward bird. I see

some brief connection, maybe. Some small joy,
stupid as sleep, yet perfect as the dream
one never can remember. Getting up,
I tangle with my bathrobe — slippers fit —
and mumble to myself the morning's prayer.

Arriving

We're newcomers to an old place. The house
was built in 1860 (so we think);
since then, the Portuguese fishermen
and the faded, artsy bohemians
have come and started now to go, replaced
by "guppies" driving Lexuses. Our street
is lined with lindens, home to chickadees
that play in the elaborate display
of whirligigs, birdbaths, wind chimes, and what's
got to be the world's most complex bird feeder
constructed by the man who lived next door
year-round, until at eighty-eight he died
of what the rumors say was "just pneumonia."
Being doctors, we are privy to much more
than other weekenders with second homes:
we know about the prostate three doors down;
across the street, it's diabetic feet
and cataracts. Some friends who've seen our place
have asked us when another like it might
become available; we sipped our drinks
beneath the twilit sky, approving of
the light, the certain quality it has
that no one could articulate. Ice clinked
as if in harmony with the cascade
of notes from those wind chimes next door; I knew
the realtors had been there yesterday.
Another neighbor down the street has AIDS,
as if to prove us not so different —
"They told me I could live with it," he'd said,

"for twenty years — and now I get lymphoma,"
while well-fed birds bounced from above like balls
belonging to the gods' unruly children.
Arriving here, perhaps like us he thought
he might escape; perhaps he sought the light
the artists and the Portuguese came here
to venerate in each their human way.
Expatriates like them, I want to say . . .
A painting we admired on a cold day,
off-season, on Commercial Street: two men
working nets in a small boat, churning sea,
the light between them captured perfectly,
belonging, it would seem, to everyone.
We left the gallery and headed home.

Absolution

The moon rises over the willow tree.
It looks like an aspirin in the sky,
bright white pill for all the world's ailments. I
remember Nonna at age eighty-three

refusing to take all her medicine.
She said she'd rather be read to in bed,
an old-fashioned love story, or instead
an article from *Reader's Digest*. When

my uncle found her one morning, her face
in halves, one peaceful and the other slack,
the doctor said she'd had a major stroke.
Two white pills sat there on a china plate,

just like the ones you bring me now. The night
is like this headache I can't shake, so full
of shapeless troubles: brave young soldiers killed,
the rising price of crude, gay marriage rights,

and worst of all, my fear of losing you.
"Doctors make the worst patients," you declare,
which sounds like something she would say before
she lost her words. Like her, I want a few

good moments rooting for my hero to
return, I want a happy ending. "No,"
I say, and push the pills away. You go,
the moon outside our window bathing you

in what seems, briefly, the absence of pain.

On Doctoring

for Thomas L. Delbanco, M.D.

A day like any other: 8 AM
and I am listening to him explain

exactly where the pain is — that it hurts
to bend the knee, especially the part

beneath the scar from where the surgeon scraped
out all the cartilage. A paper drape

provides its square of modesty (or tries
to, anyway; his boxer shorts have stripes,

blue ones, I notice half-distractedly) —
I move the joint for him, a gentle sweep

through its full range of motion. Marvelous,
the body's workmanship, how perfect is

its service to the soul it shelters, each
soft hair along the shin enshrining touch,

this way we're made to need another's care.
An awkward shifting, a throat is cleared —

enough, to realize this truth. I draw
the curtain with a screech, and glimpse the dawn

give over to the day. Like any other,
my patient gives the gift of how we suffer.

Sick Day

The clinking of recyclables picked up
accompanies an unheard benediction.
The magnetism of new passengers
pulls the heavy bus from traffic; God, how
particularly orange is this glass
of juice, so sweet it teaches us salvation.
Bell tower of a church, O pinnacle
beneath which she fed pigeons yesterday,
continue your protection of the weak,
uphold the sky, make her in her black shawl
like Grandmother's seem beautiful to me
again. We all get sick and die, we all
remember something as it happened once,
the way the houses' roofs across the street
can seem like books are closing slowly on
the stories of those inside. Holy, holy,
holy Lord, it is February, weeks
from when the sun will blaze like Florida,
hours before *Angels in America*
comes on again. What is left to be said,
the distant war like humankind's first holler
in the desert — do not leave us alone! —
when all we have are these imperfect bodies?
Feed a fever, starve a cold: still, we hunger,
so we pray with our sore throats *Grant us peace*.

Rafael Campo is a practicing physician and associate professor of medicine at Harvard Medical School. His other volumes of poetry are *Landscape with Human Figure* (Duke); *Diva* (Duke), which was nominated for the 2000 National Book Critics Circle Award; *What the Body Told* (Duke), which was awarded a 1996 Lambda Literary Award; and *The Other Man was Me: A Voyage to the New World*. He is also the author of a collection of essays, *The Poetry of Healing: A Doctor's Education in Empathy, Identity, and Desire*, which received a Lambda Literary Award in 1997.

Library of Congress Cataloging-in-Publication Data
Campo, Rafael.
The enemy / Rafael Campo.
p. cm.
ISBN-13: 978-0-8223-3862-8 (acid-free paper)
ISBN-13: 978-0-8223-3960-1 (pbk. : acid-free paper)
I. Title.
PS3553.A4883E54 2007
811'.54—dc22   2006035575